THE LAWYER.

THE LAWYER:

THE DIGNITY, DUTIES,

AND

Responsibilities of His Profession.

BY

RICHARD B. KIMBALL.

NEW-YORK:

GEORGE P. PUTNAM & COMPANY.

1853.

PREFACE.

THE Law Institute, a society composed of the most distinguished members of the legal profession in this city, determined last year to have delivered a course of lectures on subjects immediately connected with the theory, practice, and uses of the law, and the duties, proprieties, and amenities of its professors. The first lecture was given by the eminent and venerable Ogden Edwards; the writer of the following pages was honored with an application to deliver the second. This application was complied with, although a press of business prevented that attention to the subject selected, which its importance, and such an audience, demanded, and the public journals of the following day contained an ample report of what was very kindly received, from the author, by the

Institute. For copies of the lecture, frequent applications have been made ; it is therefore, to gratify some friends, reprinted, but without the author having had any time or opportunity to give it a revision.

NewYork.March1 1853.

THE LAWYER.

ALMOST since the world began, Divinity, Medicine and Law claimed *divisum imperium* in the affairs of men, until they came to be denominated, *par excellence*, the LEARNED PROFESSIONS. So ancient a division, and one which has been preserved through every change of empire and government, must certainly have had its origin in the very constitution of things. Man has always regarded, with awe and reverence, the relations he holds to his Maker. And the priest, whose duty it is to examine and expound those relations, naturally furnished the first example of a class of men set apart as a profession. Our mortal nature has always been liable to disease and accident; so that the study of medicine was another great necessity, and this produced a second learned class, denominated physicians. The health of man's soul, and the health of his body, were certainly matters of the greatest importance ; but to enjoy these something else was necessary—security,

security for person and for property. For in the earliest period of human history (and it is strange that infidel writers labor so hard to establish a man's right to the labor of his hands, when we have here so clear a statement of it), we find the Creator bestowing Eden and its appurtenances, with the reservation of one tree only, on Adam, and on his seed after him.

Thus, at the creation, were recognized those fundamental rights: the right of personal security, of personal liberty, and of property ; and this gave rise to the third of the learned professions—the Profession of the Law. For, most unhappily, notwithstanding the revelation of God's will, that men should deal justly and love mercy, we find from the very beginning of human experience, injustice and cruelty, strife and perfidious emulation abounding every where. The son of the first man was a murderer, and thence was there an immediate necessity for a criminal code. Abraham and Lot were involved in a controversy between their respective servants, about some pasture lands probably—a controversy happily terminated by the generous suggestions of the former ; thus was presented an early opportunity for an action of trespass *quare clausum*. At any rate, the great question of *meum* and *tuum* had already begun to agitate the world; and offences against the person, and violations of the right of property, have continued ever since to agitate it.

The truth is, injuries and revenges form, in series, a great part of the world's history ; so that from the very first, there has been an absolute necessity for wise laws and a proper administration of them. In this respect, we owe more to a remote antiquity than we are apt to imagine. I do not refer to the introduction of what is called the common law in England, nor indeed to any period since the Christian era. I recall the time immediately subsequent to the flood, which may be termed the second creation,—

> " When the world looked as it were fresh and young,
>   And the great deluge still had left it green."

It has been much the fashion with historians to descant eloquently on the gradual processes by which man, from an ignorant and almost brutal savage, without language, without laws, almost without any thing which should distinguish him from the basest series in animated nature, approximated by slow degrees, and at last attained perfectly to his present refinement, dignity, and intellectual, moral, and material elevation.

Gentlemen, man, as a race, never was in such a condition, and never " worked up " from such a condition. There have been always savage clans, wandering, turbulent and fierce, and their numbers are still great, scattered over different parts of the earth ; but they compose a class which, having retrograded from their

1*

first estate, formed themselves into wild tribes, who have always been opposed to any change of condition, and we fail to find evidence in history that any considerable portion of them have ever been humanized; on the contrary, like the North American Indians, they have gradually retired before the advance of civilized peoples, sinking deeper and deeper into barbarism and brutality till they have been lost in fusion or extinction. No history is so ancient that it does not refer to and describe these savage hordes. The Hebrew speaks of such —so does the Egyptian—so does the Greek—and so does the Roman; and you will bear in mind that in the first accounts we have of man after the flood, he is seen in magnificent cities, with a knowledge of the arts and mechanical skill, which, in some respects, has never since been equalled. There are no annals so remote in the past that we do not find in them laws promulgated, and justice, in some measure and form, administered; and, in this connection, I come more particularly to the subject of—the Profession and Practice of the Law.

This subject does not properly embrace any history of the enactment of different laws, or a consideration of special acts, or of what may be called the study and knowledge of the law. Yet it will be impossible not to make occasional reference to these matters in the practical observations I propose on a class who profess and practise law.

It is an interesting inquiry, and it may not be an
uninstructive one, to ascertain at what period the trial,
or hearing, of causes was instituted, and whether the
office of an advocate is coeval with it. It has been re-
marked, by an eminent English writer, that, "in the
infancy of the earth, when laws were few and patriarchs
judges, every man was his own lawyer, and needed not
an attorney to write or an advocate to plead for him:
but himself demanded at the hands of the judge what
of right he deemed his own. Afterwards, when king-
doms became vast, and laws many, and the forms of law
complicated, and the administration of laws tedious,
labor divided. Hence arose advocates, barristers, attorneys, &c." I confess, in examining the subject, I
cannot discover a period when advocates did not exist.

The Book of Job is admitted by philologists to be
the most ancient volume extant. The period of which it
treats was that of Abraham. It abounds in phrases
which show not only a regular administration of justice,
but speak also of the labors of third parties, who ap-
peared on behalf of the petitioner, or of the accused.
"Judges" are mentioned; particular laws are referred
to; and such expressions are used as "the trial of the
innocent"—"thou renewest thy witnesses against me"
—"coming together to trial"—"a daysman"—"an
arbitrator between us"—"pleading the cause of the
poor," and "the intercessor;" from all which we are

bound to infer, that either on the one side or the other, it was even then the habit to seek the assistance of an "advocate."

For the benefit of our brethren professing the science of medicine, I might remark, by way of digression, that in looking through the Book of Job to support the claims of the bar to antiquity, I encountered a text which showed conclusively that they had an equally remote origin, although there must have been a vast improvement in the science since those days. The verse, I confess, does not reflect very great credit on the then existing faculty: "Ye are all physicians of no value;" but it showed the existence of the profession at that time.

It was frequently the case, doubtless, in those ancient days, for both the plaintiff and the defendant to plead his own cause; still, as in this way sides would scarcely ever be equally balanced, one party having more eloquence, or influence, or friends, than the other, it will be at once seen that the office of advocate did not arise so much in consequence of the increasing complication of the laws, rendering a division of labor necessary, as, from the very constitution of things, by which a man required the assistance of his fellow, against the superior influence or eloquence of some other whom he deemed his oppressor, and against whom he sought to enforce a right, or to resist the enforcement of what he considered a wrong. Thus you will perceive that I would vindicate our profession from the charge of being instituted after society and laws became so complicated that it was necessary to employ a class of men who should exist by their subtlety and shrewdness, and who are necessary evils. On the contrary, I maintain that as man is constituted, the advocate is as necessary as the law, and that his office is founded in mercy and in benevolence.

The Egyptians are said to have been the first people who rightly understood the rules of government, and their country was considered by the ancients as the most renowned school for politics, and the source whence the arts and sciences were derived. As a nation, they were grave and serious, and they bestowed their noblest labors on the intellectual improvement of mankind, so that Stephen, when praising Moses, says of him, " he was learned in all the wisdom of the Egyptians."

In the Egyptian courts, affairs were transacted entirely by writing, in order to guard against surprise, and to prevent the effect of what was termed false eloquence, which dazzles the mind and moves the passions. It was declared that truth could not be expressed with too much plainness, as it alone was to have weight in judgments, because in that alone the rich and poor, the powerful and weak, the learned and the ignorant were to find relief and security. Thus the advocate had already begun to have recourse to improper influences, which were looked upon with disfavor by the judges, and guarded against in the way I have mentioned. I particularly call your attention to this fact, which shows how early the habits, which are charged as sins against our profession, began to creep into it, and in what light they were considered.

We come next to the Greeks, and I shall speak of the Athenians as furnishing the most prominent example of Grecian civilization and government. I can hardly refrain from alluding briefly to some of their laws, although they constitute no part of my subject. The student will be amply repaid by a close examination of these laws ; and he will be surprised to find how many are copied *verbatim* in our own statute books. For example, in criminal trials, the question put to the prisoner was literally, " Are you guilty or not guilty ? " The Athenian courts were almost as numerous as our own; process was served very nearly as it now is, that is, service was made by the bailiff, or it could be done by the plaintiff himself, provided he had a witness present ; this was a citation to appear on a certain day before the judge. If the suit was against a married woman, the husband had to be joined. Before the trial of a cause, both parties were obliged to deposit in court a certain sum (a sort of security for costs), depending on the amount in litigation, and regulated by it. This, after the determination of the matter, was divided among the judges, and the losing party not only forfeited the amount he had deposited, but was obliged to restore the money paid by his adversary. I submit the point whether here was not the germ of the fee bill. Little, however, could the subtle Greek, with all his philosophy and imagination have fathomed the intricacies of the modern bill of costs, as made out by an English attorney, or even by a New-York solicitor, before the code. There were also circuit judges who went through a certain number of boroughs, and had cognizance of all controversies about money, when it did not exceed a certain sum. Arbitrations or references, almost precisely like our own, were common. I might allude to a vast number of their laws, such as the law for a general jail delivery—of limitations—the mode of conducting trial—nonsuits—examination of plaintiff and defendant—property exempt from execution, &c., to show how closely the moderns have followed the sages of antiquity ; but it does not come within the scope of my present purpose, and I have referred to the subject, simply to invite to it the attention of the law student. Among the Athenians I find the first account of advocates who pleaded for a fee. Sometimes the parties themselves delivered a set oration in their own behalf, which was composed by one of the orators. If they desired it, advocates were appointed to plead for them ; the doing of which was called ἐπὶ μισθῶ συνηγορεῖν—*to plead for a fee*. I would remark, that lest their orations should try the judges' patience and prevent their attending to other business, they were limited to a certain time, which was measured by an hour-glass. With the Greeks, as all know, the office of advocate and orator became one of great influence and importance. Demosthenes himself was first led to the study of eloquence for the argument of his own cause against an unjust guardian. Was there ever a time when there were not dishonest officials and knavish guardians, and in fact, defaulters of every grade and condition ?

We come next to the Romans. Among them, we find the administration of the laws reduced to an elaborate system, and the practice of law regulated by special rules, and developed quite as fully as it is at the present day. I will not seem so far to undervalue the understanding of any law student as to recommend a careful examination of the laws and judicial proceedings of the ancient Romans. Learned commentators have written volumes in praise of the civil law, and I need only say that we have scarcely a general rule or statute which is not traceable to it.

Among the Romans I first find too much importance attached to forms in pleading. The greatest caution at length came to be necessary in drawing up process, for if there was a mistake in one word the whole cause was lost. *Qui plus petebat quam debitum est, causam perdebat.* I regret to add that all this technicality, and all these petty exceptions to the forms of pleading, were chargeable on unworthy members of the profession. As is still the case every where, there were small, narrow-minded, bustling, and officious creatures of the law, who sought to prosecute and defend actions by the most reprehensible courses. These persons were (as they are still) great annoyances to the honorable lawyer. Cicero very frequently complains of them. He calls the person who is skilled only in the framing of writs and in picking flaws in pleadings, *leguleius*—a pettifogger: also, *præco actionum*—*cantor formularum*—*auceps syllabarum*—a crier of actions—a singer of forms—a caviller in syllables. So that such persons were at that day exposed to merited contempt. It was also among the Romans that we first find a systematic division of the profession into special pleaders, counsellors and advocates : the first prepared the pleadings ; the second, who were called *ministrators*, often sat by the side of the advocate to make suggestions ; the third argued the case. This was done much as it is at present, each party making two speeches : the first answering to our opening, and the second to our summing up. How many hours were to be allowed to each advocate was left for the court to determine. Hour-glasses were used, as among the Greeks. Sometimes the advocates were given as much time as they required.

Under the Emperors, a despicable custom crept in.

Certain advocates employed and kept in their pay a class of people called *mancipes* — a sort of modern *clacqueur* — whose business it was to procure persons who should attend the court and applaud, while they were speaking, whenever a man, who stood among them, should give the word. These persons received for the service a stipulated sum, generally about three denarii—some four shillings of our money—a day. I need not add that such a practice was despised and ridiculed.

With reference to the Romans, I repeat that almost all our laws, all our legal rules, our very mode of trial— jury trial and all—are derived from them.

One word as to the trial by jury. We are in the habit of referring to the enactments of Alfred for the establishment of this invaluable prerogative of the people, so that it is often called the " Englishman's privilege." The limitation of the number to twelve men, and the framing of special rules referring to the selection of the jury from the "hundred," belong to Alfred. But the Roman trials were really jury trials. The word *Judices*, in the plural, is translated "Judges," but refers to a certain number, about five hundred, who were selected for the hearing and deciding of a cause, the *Questor*, or *Prætor*, sitting as magistrate, and who were at first taken from the Patricians, and afterwards from the Equites, from which five hundred the defendant selected fifty to hear and determine the action, *until at length the "judices" in criminal cases were chosen from the people themselves.* This certainly was a trial by jury, and to the Romans is due the credit of establishing it.

Italy at length was invaded and conquered by the Goths, who were not the savage and uncivilized race many writers would have us suppose. We have the evidence of Grotius that, as a nation, they possessed great integrity, and were distinguished by love of justice and good faith, and were governed by wise laws. These laws, Eric, the Visigoth, who reigned in A. D. 470, caused to be digested into a code, which is acknowledged to be the fountain of Spanish law, and was prior, by fifty years, to the Pandects of the Roman law, made by order of Justinian. Notwithstanding this, I do not find any particular account among these northern nations of the manner in which judicial proceedings were conducted, or of the occupation, as a *profession,* of advocates. Shortly, the ordeal, or trial by fire or water, and the trial by judicial combat, which prevailed generally, struck a blow to all fair administration of justice, and to the employment of the lawyer. Under the feudal system, when the chief oppressed or defended his vassal at pleasure, and claimed both civil and criminal jurisdiction over him, there was no shelter from violence or oppression, and the arm of the brave was the only tribunal to which the helpless could appeal for security or redress. So chivalry came in place of legal administration, and knights in armor were advocates by the strong hand.

To Charlemagne is due the credit of reviving the civil administration of justice. He established a code; he caused courts to be organized, and a regular system to be established for the hearing or trial of causes, in which a business-like order prevailed, and the advocate once more was called to exercise his proper functions. A few years later, Alfred, in England, framed the code, which, although now lost, is so well known by every student to be the basis of English jurisprudence; and from this period we may trace a steady improvement in legal administration, and also the revival of our profession. A wonderful impetus was given to both by the discovery of the Pandects, at Amalfi, in the twelfth century; the code was thereafter studied with eagerness, and professors of civil law were appointed, who taught it throughout Europe. Lawyers, once more eloquent and learned, were heard sustaining or defending clients, until the profession and practice of the law reached its present importance and responsibility. Omitting any notice of the changes, which, from time to time, have taken place in the modern history of the profession, and which are generally familiar, I come directly to the duties of the lawyer at the present day, and the relations which, in my opinion, he holds to society. A lawyer, according to the definition of a distinguished writer, "is the servant of his fellow-men, for the attainment of justice, in which is expressed both the lowliness and the dignity of his calling: the lowliness—in that he is the servant of all, ever ready to assist as well the meanest as the loftiest; the dignity—in that the end whereto he serves has, among things temporal, no superior or equal." This definition I understand to include all who are properly members of our profession: the advocate—the chamber counsel—the conveyancer, and the general practitioner in or out of court; and I shall in these remarks use the term "lawyer" in this general sense.

There are certain charges habitually raised against the profession, which have ordinarily been treated with contempt as vulgar opinions or errors, but which, nevertheless, can be traced to the conduct of base advocates and base attorneys. Sundry low witticisms and jests are current also, having for their mark the members of the bar; and while we feel these to be altogether below our notice, we cannot disguise the truth, that miserable creatures of our own profession have given rise to them. For the higher and the more honorable the pursuit, the more despicable and degraded are those who pervert and misuse it. The greater the opportunity for acting the peacemaker and settling a difficulty, the viler must be his character who stirs up strife instead, and who glories in promoting contention. So far, then, as the true profession and practice of the law is noble, so far is the counterfeit utterly base and contemptible. A low attorney has nothing lower to be compared with. While I would honor the vocation of the lawyer, may I be permitted to point out some difficulties and temptations which beset the path of those about to enter on it.

The world, most unhappily, is in a state of antagonism. Buyer and seller, employer and employee, master and servant, debtor and creditor, hold perpetual petty contests; occupations and trades conflict, sects come into collision with sects, statesmen raise cries against statesmen, and politician strives to circumvent politician; the priest vents his anathema against priest, and physician abuses physician. In short, repulsive as is the picture, the world seems filled with a perpetual and unceasing strife. And the definition given by a German author to the principle of evil—I am the spirit that still *resists*—would seem to be proved true by the very state of things. In this unvarying and ceaseless contest the lawyer is continually appealed to. One desires, by securing his aid, to make him the instrument of his revenge: another seeks in him protection from revenge: a third puts his life in his hands, and entreats that he would save it: a fourth trusts to him to defend a reputation dearer than life, while a fifth implores him to save his property, often held dearer than reputation. Questions of legislation, of corporate rights and franchises, church difficulties, family difficulties, and personal difficulties of every kind, are brought before the lawyer in the ordinary discharge of his vocation. Indeed, the whole machinery of affairs, from the most important to the most trivial, must come under his observation, and be, in a measure, regulated by his advice. What a field for good! What ample opportunity for wickedness! What a scope for the exercise of his calling as a servant of his fellow-men for the attainment of justice! What range for every variety of mischief! The lawyer has the power to do more good than the priest, because his efforts are practical and in an area where the latter does not enter. Unhappily the power proves too often a stumbling-block—a temptation—and he sinks to the use of unworthy means for unworthy purposes.

I do not propose to dwell on, but simply to touch the vexed subject of what is called "legal morality," so frequently canvassed and discussed by casuists, and revived from time to time, as some incident in a trial brings it prominently before the public. This is commonly resolved into the charge against our profession of defending a cause which the advocate knows to be wrong, or a prisoner whom he knows to be guilty. Under this head, one of the most striking examples is the defence by Phillips, of Courvoisier, on trial for murder, in 1840.

Courvoisier confessed his guilt to his counsel on the second day of his trial, and yet insisted the defence should be continued, and begged Mr. Phillips to do all he could to save him. The affair, at the time, created a great deal of excitement, and this has recently been revived, whereupon the question was once more elaborately discussed in the English journals, and particularly in the London Law Magazine. Numerous opinions were given, of every shade and complexion. The most startling was certainly contained in a quotation made by Mr. Phillips himself, in defending his conduct, from Lord Brougham's statement, at the trial of Queen Caroline, of the duties of an advocate. What should strike every one as most remarkable in this discussion is, that all sides, by tacit consent, seemed to admit that there were certain rules of legal morality, not applicable to other persons, by which the profession should be judged, and that the only question was, whether Mr. Phillips had exceeded them. Lord Brougham says :*

" An advocate, by the sacred duties which he owes his client, knows, in the discharge of that office, but one

---

* To show how general is this theory of the advocate's duties, we subjoin the following extracts;

" There are falsehoods which are not lies, that is, which are not criminal; as, 1, where no one is deceived, which is the case in parables, fables, novels, jests, tales to create mirth, ludicrous embellishments of a story, where the declared design of a speaker is not to in-person in the world,—that client and none other. To save that client by all expedient means, to protect that client at all hazards and cost to all others, and, among

form but to divert; compliments in the subscription of a letter, a servant's denying his master, a prisoner pleading not guilty, *and an advocate asserting the justice of his belief of the justice of his client's cause.* In such instances no confidence is destroyed, because none was reposed; no promise to speak the truth is violated, because none was given or understood to be given."—*Paley's Moral Philosophy. Chapter on " Lies."*

" BOSWELL : But, Sir, does not affecting warmth when you have no warmth, and appearing to be clearly of one opinion when you are in reality of another opinion, does not such dissimulation impair one's honesty ? Is there not some danger that a Lawyer may put on the same mask in common life in the intercourse with his friends ? JOHNSON : Why no, Sir ; *everybody knows you are paid for affecting warmth for your client,* and it is therefore properly no dissimulation ; the moment you come from the bar you resume your usual behaviour. Sir, a man will no more carry the artifice of the bar into the common intercourse of society, than a man who is paid for tumbling upon his hands when he should walk on his feet."—*Boswell's Life of Johnson.*

We will not at present inquire whether the doctrine which is held on this subject by English Lawyers be or be not agreeable to reason or morality ;—whether it be right that a man should, with a wig on his head, and a band round his neck, do for a guinea what without these appendages he would think it wicked and infamous to do for an empire ;—whether it be right, that not merely believing, but knowing, a statement to be true, he should do all that can be done by sophistry, by rhetoric, by solemn asseveration, by indignant exclamation, by gesture, by play of features, by terrifying one honest witness, by perplexing another, to cause a jury to think that statement false. It is

other things, to himself, is the highest and most un-
questioned of his duties ; he must not regard the alarm,
the suffering, the torment, the destruction which he may
bring on any other."

A more monstrous doctrine, I do not hesitate to say,

not necessary on the present occasion to decide these questions. *The
professional rules, be they good or bad, are rules to which many wise and
virtuous men have conformed, and are daily conforming. If, therefore,
Bacon did no more than these rules required of him, we shall readily admit that he was blameless."*—Article on Montagu's defence of Lord Bacon.
vol. 65.—*Edinburgh Review.*

" As an orator he was an advocate for his client, or more properly
personated him. Here then without question he was to *feign* and *dis-
semble* his own opinions and to speak those of his client. And though
some of those who call themselves *casuists,* have held it unlawful for
an advocate to defend what he thinks an ill cause, yet I apprehend it
to be the natural right of every member of society, whether accusing
or accused, to speak freely and fully for himself. And if, either by
a legal or natural incapacity, this cannot be done in *person,* to have a
proxy provided or allowed by the state, to do for him what he cannot
or may not do for himself."—*Bishop Warburton.*

" The statements by opposite Advocates may not be most bene-
ficial to the practitioner ; and as the Advocate may profess feelings
which he does not feel, and may support a cause which he knows to
be wrong : as it is a species of acting without an avowal that it is acting ; it may appear at variance with some of our best feelings. It is
however, nothing but appearance. The Advocate is in reality an
officer assisting in the administration of justice, and acting under the
impression that truth is elicited and difficulties disentangled by the
opposite statements of able men. He is only troubling the waters
that they may exert their virtues.—*Basil Montague.*

was never broached. It is *this* which has actually lowered the profession and practice of the law in the estimation of the people—and the day has gone by when one may look with contempt on that opinion. The *practices* of a few disreputable persons could not bring disgrace on a whole body : but the avowal, by leading members of that body, of this doctrine of " legal .morality," and the practising under it, *has* cast disrepute over the legal character; it has brought the lawyer to be viewed in the low light of a paid actor, to whose assertion, unsupported by proof or reference, no credit was to be attached. How often have we heard jurymen address counsel, after the verdict had been recorded, " Well, now that it is all over, what is your *real* opinion on that point ? " Surely an advocate must feel humiliated by such a question ; and it *is* humiliating that any of our brethren—men of education and of strong minds, should so far forget not only what they owe to a noble profession, but what is due to themselves, as to be satisfied with the petty triumph of obtaining a verdict against evidence, by a dexterous concealment of the facts, or a skilful perversion of them. There is no such thing—there ought to be no such thing as the morality of the advocate, as distinguished from the morality of the man. All that the advocate can assume, either in criminal or civil cases, is to be clothed with the rights and duties of his client. That client has no right to fabricate, to prevaricate, or to falsify, for the sake of a defence; neither has the advocate a right to do it for him. The most that can be maintained, with regard to the advocate's labors, is that he is engaged in trying to find all the evidence of the truth on one side—his opponent seeking similar evidence on the opposite : while the judge and jury, by putting the two sides together, are enabled to get at the whole truth. Falsehood is no element of determining: and to pretend that an advocate is at the command (and for money) of a confessed felon, or an admitted swindler, is to accept a very low position for the bar. In short, an advocate has no right to say or do for his client what he would not say and do for himself; and as he would not, if a true man, either misstate or mystify, color or conceal, in his own behalf—how can he do these things in behalf of another ? *

* It is most satisfactory to know that in earlier periods the doctrine of " legal morality " found no recognition from the court or legislature.

By the Roman law the advocates in each case were obliged, at the commencement of it, to swear upon the Holy Evangelists, that they would defend with all their force what they should judge to be true and just; and that they would abandon the defence of any cause which they should find in the beginning to be unjust, or which in the progress they should discover to be unjust. " Patroni autem causarum, qui utrique parti suum præstantes auxilium ingrediuntur, cum lis fuerit contestata, post narrationem propositam, et contradictionem objectam, in qualicunque judicio majore vel minore, vel apud arbitros,

There is probably no city of the United States where there is so little of the *esprit du corps* among the members of the legal profession as in our own. A short sojourn in Boston or Philadelphia, will convince one how much more it prevails in those places than with us. This is owing to the all-engrossing sway of mercantile influence which pervades and controls all classes and conditions of men in the Great Emporium,

sive ex compromisso sive aliter datos vel electos, sacrosanctis Evangeliis tactis, juramentum præstant quod omni quidem virtute suâ, omnique ope, quod verum et justum existimaverint clientibus suis inferre procurabunt, nihil studii relinquentes quod sibi possibile est; non autem creditâ sibi causâ cognitâ quod improba sit vel penitus desperata, et ex mendacibus allegationibus composita ipsi scientes prudentesque malâ conscientiâ liti patrocinabuntur, sed et si certamine procedente aliquid tale sibi cognitum fuerit à causa recedent ab hujusmodi communione sese penitus separantes."—*Col. l.* 14.; § 1 *de Judic.*

The ancient law of Scotland required, that "Advocates in the time of their admission, *and yearly*, should be sworn to execute their office of advocation diligently and truly; and that as soon as they understand their client's cause to be unjust or wrongful, that they should incontinent leave the same, and desist from all further pursuit or defence."—*Statute of the Lords*, 13th June, 1537.

The law of Spain requires an oath from advocates, "That they will conduct themselves faithfully, and will not defend unjust causes." —*Institutes of the Civil Law of Spain*, by D. Ignatius Jordan de Asso y del Reo, and D. Miguel de Manuel y Rodriguez.

Vide Appendix to *The Lawyer*, by Edward O'Brien. London: 1842.

2*

and to which I grieve to say even our own profession is in a measure subject. Commerce brings wealth in its train, and wealth commands all things : so that the personality of the legal profession seems to be swallowed up in the vortex. Our merchants are apt to look upon a lawyer as a kind of intellectual gladiator, whose business it is to do battle for a consideration in any cause imaginable—a sort of civil Dugald Dalgetty—scrupulously faithful to his retainer till the service is ended, and then up for a new market. Gentlemen, it is our own fault if our clients so regard us : and let it be our part immediately to undeceive them. The fact is, that too often with lawyer and client the proper order of things is entirely reversed. The client calls upon the lawyer to have a certain thing done, instead of to be instructed what it is best for him to do. The only question would seem to be with persons of this class, "Is it practicable ? " assuming that if it *is*, there can be no impediment. We sometimes hear the lawyer excusing a severe course toward an unfortunate party, by saying " his instructions are peremptory." One would suppose this to be the language of some mere agent doing the work of his principal, instead of that of an educated member of a learned profession, whose vocation it is to advise and to direct. I trust I shall be understood as pointing out the shoals and quicksands which encompass the lawyer—not as making a general charge against a profession, whose office I do not hesitate to extol and magnify. Still, I think the evils to which I allude are seriously increasing, and, as I have observed, their cure belongs to us.

I know that to the young attorney especially, who is just commencing in the world, and who, perhaps, has struggled with difficulties and begins his profession without means, and who must in consequence have immediate occupation, it is hard to take exceptions to the conduct of a client who brings him his first cause, although he should dictate to him a course which he would blush to follow. Yet the young attorney *must* resist. He must reflect that there is no occupation so despicable as that which undertakes to conduct chicaneries and intrigues at second-hand. He must ask himself, " Can I do this and preserve my self-respect?" He must reject with scorn all patronage proffered him as the instrument of injustice. Let him remember that the question should be, not how much he can make out of his profession, but how he can best adorn it. Let him hold out with this idea unto the end, and he shall have his reward.

I cannot close these hastily-composed observations without alluding to one thing which I believe, in this State, worked an almost irreparable injury to the position of the legal profession. I refer to the old fee bill, by which on default in an action for the collection of a debt, an exorbitant sum was adjudged to the practitioner for a trifling service—a service which an ordinary clerk could perform after having been six weeks in a law office—the nature of this fee bill being such that, by the ingenuity of attorneys, and solicitors, and taxing officers, it grew year by year till it fell under the merited rebuke of the whole people. In it was a direct encouragement to the lowest order of legal attainment, and a direct discouragement of high professional merit. The young man who could pass examination and come to the city, and make the acquaintance of even but one or two jobbing houses, and get their collecting business, was comfortably provided for at the start, and had nothing to do but to go on and prosper. Our State came to be considered the paradise of attorneys—for in no other in the Union were any such rewards held within the reach of men of as mean abilities, and such unscrupulous morality. But at length, happily for the honor of the profession, the fee bill was abolished.

The mere collection of an undisputed claim is not the business of the lawyer. I do not say that he can avoid it altogether—as it is impossible always to foresee in what cases defences may be interposed. Yet in our minor courts, individuals find no difficulty in attending to their own collections, and calling in the aid of an attorney if the case prove to be litigated. I repeat, the mere collection of debts—that shrewd and adroit management by which a client's demand is secured from some miserable, perhaps dishonest debtor, while other creditors, equally entitled, get nothing; that cunning, overreaching alertness, ready with surprises and stratagems, to extort what the law itself has guarded; that apt knowledge of forms and routines, and of every technicality used in collecting machinery; all these are no part of the profession or practice of the law. They belong—if they belong anywhere—to the constable and the bailiff, and should have no more connection with the legal profession, than the office of hereditary hangman had with that of the judge. Yet to such a degree, it must be confessed, do persons admitted to practise in the courts, occupy themselves with these base uses of their offices, that the lawyer, instead of the eminent dignity to which he is entitled by his legitimate pursuits and fit accomplishments, is held to occupy, in the opinion of many, almost the least honorable of all the places in society.

But the field of the law is very wide, without exploring any such territory, and the lawyer in his vocation has need to husband himself for the real duties of his calling. For, as has been finely expressed, all men, in all places, and at all times, stand in need of justice, and, of necessity, of the advice of those who are learned in the law, and who give life and motion to justice. By it each has, from all others, that which is his due; to sustain it governments have been ordained, while society